All These Little Things

Dhriti Parashar

BookLeaf
Publishing

India | USA | UK

Presentation by *BookLeaf Publishing*

Web: www.bookleafpub.com

E-mail: info@bookleafpub.com

ISBN: 9789360948245

First edition 2024

DEDICATION

To my schoolmates

PREFACE

"Be yourself; everyone else is already taken."

-Oscar Wilde

Walls

It's been years
I have been saying the same thing
But nobody wants to listen
Does the truth hurt so much?

Amidst glistening tears
Poor souls have met their fate
It's still not too late
But the world is such

That the voices will remain suppressed
Whoever wants to come out and stand

Is pushed underneath the dust
And division has become a must.

You and I can't sit on the same seats
Can't wear the same clothes
Can't go to the same places
Can't study in the same schools.

Not all are allowed to work
Not all are allowed to love
And the world is such
That division has forcefully been made a must.

It's high time we realize
Mankind needs to flourish
And the only way to bridge
Is to break the walls.

The walls behind which women have been caged
The walls behind which religions stand enraged
The walls because of which negativity has
increased
The walls which when broken are destined to
make peace.

Best Among Equals

Welcome to the jungle!
Kings change here everyday,
You can't trust a soul,
To lead you to your prey.

So before you become one yourself,
A bit of an advice,
Buckle your shoes, gear up while you're at it
So you're prepared to thrive.

The top line is what
Everyone is aiming for
The competitive feeling full of rebut
Fills the hearts of even the pure.

There'll be loads of tyranny
You see what is the irony

Even the best and gifted are weak
If they don't work to maintain their streak.

All eyes are on you
Waiting for you to fail
But you'll have to show them
You're strong and not frail.

The Fallen Hero

The fallen leaf
Unmasked the grief
It is okay for the greatest ones to cry.
But the fallen ones will try
Try again, till their throat goes dry.

Rising up from the dust
To reach the mountains
They'll shove off the rust
They'll break the chains.

The ones who have made it
Know what it takes

For the fallen hero
To bet against the stakes.

People will say, but who's listening
His excellence would end his silence
He'll have to prove himself again
The world is not known for compliance.

The hero is not fallen
Until he himself believes it
Until he accepts there is no way back.
The fallen ones can rise again
Reach to the top from the crack.

Polaroid

The first day in school
Everybody stared at me
Like they had seen a ghost
So we didn't talk much.

I was trying hard to memorize names
Make new friends and not be lame
So I cracked a couple of bad jokes
To entertain the new folks.

Months passed, it felt like home
Seemed like I had been there for years
There were people I began to know inside out
I realized life had changed gears.

Too quick, the days went by
With the memories we had built
The storehouse of souvenirs
We had built brick by brick.

And had gotten attached too much to let go
End of the day what was left, were polaroids
Of our endless dreams and countless scenes
We sketched during our friendship
That turned so deep
Too valuable to let 'em slip.

Don't Worry!

If you get wet in the rain,
And have to run back home,
If your landlord kicks you out of the house
And for the night on the streets you roam,
Don't worry, just smile
Tomorrow will bring new hope
A chance for you to cope,
Be sure to do it in style.

If you can't solve your homework quite right,
If your friends ditch you on party night,
Don't worry, you'll be alright
Enjoy with yourself,
It can still be a movie night.

If your mom tells you, 'you don't score well'
And you feel you are dumb, in a nutshell
Don't worry, you can still excel
Take a break, don't stay up late
Don't rake your brain like hell.

If you got a problem with somebody
Don't try to break his head
Even if you want to beat 'em up
Just smile instead
And don't worry, be happy.

Backseat Driving

Four people in the car
Too adamant to use their brains
And 5 kms becomes too far
The driver's training goes in vain.

The sixty-five-year-old
Knows everything so well
But says 'Turn to the right'
When he's pointing to the left.

The fourteen-year-old
Is in his early teenage years
So he won't leave the phone
Until everybody hears.

He wants to give advice
Using his little knowledge of streets
He knows his driving skills are better
He learnt it in his dreams.

The mother holds the map upside-down
As they stop at the traffic light
Realizes they'll have to turn around
Cover double the distance, at 11 in the night.

So Inertia-tic

My mom told me to go and make some friends
So I logged into my Instagram account
She said I should go outside and play
But I was too busy sitting and passing the day.

You see I am resting
I don't want to move
I'm having a good time
Staring into thin air
Like I don't care
And I don't know what to do.

I don't remember telling you
I've been off the tennis court for months
And now I am too afraid
That my arms hesitate
So I prefer to not play.

I ate my breakfast in bed
Aiming to skip the lunch altogether
'Cause I'm too sleepy to get up
And it seems like forever
Since I last went out
To breathe in the fresh air
Wearing a new shirt and my Denim
My inertia has gained momentum.

What Do You Care?

Is my hair a bit too short?
Is my nose a bit too long?
Am I slim or really not?
Is this where I really belong?

None of this
I say,
None of this is going
to make a difference.

Cause you are right where you need to be
Right when you should get started
Right when you prepare to win
Go all out and not half-hearted.

Only the work you do
Is what will make the difference
Not the fact that your eyes are blue
Neither your looks, nor your appearance.

It's Been The Same

They'll call a seventeen-year-old, a baby
When you want to learn how to drive a car
They'll say you are not old enough
No matter how big you are.

But when you move your house
And they want the new one to get rid of dirt
They'll say you're a grown-up now
And giving a hand won't hurt.

So parents are so indecisive
They just can't decide
If you are big or small
And they'll change their opinion
Just like the color of the chameleon
Depends on what you ask for
Or what they want to get done.

Gone

Should I compare this feeling
To a cold winter evening
When I am old and all alone.

And I know I can't stop you,
It wasn't that big an issue
But I'll have to let it go.

Now the rains would come by
And the stars would shine bright
But I'd have no one to
Dance away the night.

You shut your eyes tight
Said there's no going back
Who am I to tell you to stay?

You've changed a someone who
You loved more than anyone
To a someone you don't want around.

But you mean too much to me
If you tell me to leave
I will go away without a sound.

Secret Ingredient

You are exactly who you need to be
There is no master key
The only thing to make anything special
Is to believe.

The sea is never afraid
It can never be contained
It masters its abilities
Exploring possibilities.

There is no set way for how things should be
There is always room for creativity
You don't have to change yourself
For how others think you should be.

For something to become special
You need to believe it is special
The day you recognize your limitless power
You'll find the road to the tallest tower.

Roses aren't always red
The sky isn't always blue
The only secret ingredient
You need, is YOU.

Teenage

Some days you'll feel bored
When you are left alone in your room
On other days you'd want to be ignored
And feel annoyed when talked to.

You'll feel the urgent need to color your hair
And to become a trendsetter
Sometimes you'd be conscious of what you
should wear
But you'd have friends, around whom you won't
care.

Fangirling over a new band would be normal
Buying their merchandise would become a must
Attending concerts would be the ultimate dream
But in everyday regime, you'd have to adjust.

You'd become better schemers
To sneak out with friends
And great day-dreamers
Lost in their own world.

You'd want to make a point
You'd want everyone to hear
You'd be upset if they don't
It's called 'teenage', my dear!

Diamonds

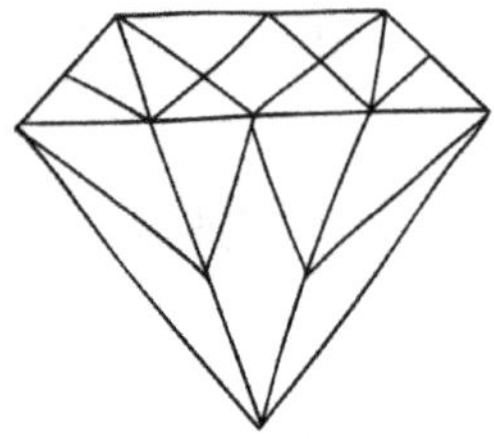

Many pieces of glass are cut
But how many make it through the heat?
How many withstand the test of time,
To survive and reach their prime.

It is not any glass that is chosen
To make the rings we wear
Only the ones that are deemed fit
Those that don't break,
Stand with perseverance and grit.

Not all pieces of glass shine alike
Not all are called gems
And you'll see the brightest ones
They're not just glass but diamonds.

The fragile and weak are thrown away,
Only the strong are defined.
Only the hardest and brightest diamonds
Survive to reach their prime.

Mischief

You're supposed to be a good kid
But all of it seems a bad bid
If you are asked to follow the rules
The boring ones set by schools.

It's hard to be what you're not
And creativity gets rot
If you stop making mischiefs
From blowing up toilets to hiding handkerchiefs.

Not everyone needs to save the world
Some of us can create trouble
And think outside the box
To get out of your bubble.

Before

I've become a young woman
Running to reach somewhere
But the fragrance of flowers
On the side paths takes me home.

I've outgrown my little dresses
I've moved to a new city
There's nothing like the picket fences
We'd painted so pretty.

A busy shopping complex
Has replaced the park
Where I strolled
Listening to music in the dark.

They say the streets are the same everywhere
But these sidewalks aren't that green
The traffic lights are unnecessarily mean
And there's no sign of grumpy Mrs. Blaire.

Let There Be No Excuse!

"It's an open window
But I never was taught to fly
I don't have wings for aid
Nor the will to try.

Had I only been taught how to run faster,
I could have reached early
Had I only been taught to focus better,
I could have proved myself worthy."

"O' come out of this delusion, child
You don't need wings to learn to fly,
But you do need determination
To soar high in the sky.

Nobody would help you
Until you help yourself, and you know it
It's time you learn from your mistake
And begin to own it.

Nobody will teach you how to run faster
You can only practice that
It is the fire in your belly
What will make you better.

You won't always have a GPS
To help you track your goal
It's great power that you possess
But you should know how to gain control."

Hero of My Life

I am the hero of my life
I saved myself from agony
Not a figure I despise
There's no one who I want to be.

I am the hero of my life
I gave myself the company
I needed to survive
The silence that surrounded me.

I don't wear a cloak
But I'm sure you've seen me fly
I brought myself ashore
When I was stuck in the tides.

And when the world pushed me into the dark
I bore all the weight
Until I saw a spark
Until I could see straight.

But you know there's a king maker
Behind the greatest ones
They give you the strength to be a risk taker
When all of it seems lost.

I can't deny, sure I had one
I won't just thank the ones who kept me from
fading
But also those who troubled me a ton and
Taught me the need for upgrading.

Out Of Reach

Her moves are a little rusty
She's been out of touch
It's been whole eight months
Her game's refused to release the clutch.

The last time she was on court
She was one of the best
But now it seems this is the first time
She has held her shield to the rest.

But she knows nothing's out of reach
As long as she grows
She can see it happening
She'll steal the titles in a row.

All she needs is patience and the belief
That she'll be on the top of the world
The day is not too far away
That she'll be on the top of her game
She's come and she is here to stay.

She'll work day in and out
If she has to, to make sure
She stays ahead of the crowd
She knows nothing will work out
If she starts looking for an easy way out
The only way out is the way through,
An easier option was never made
For the ones who desire to win
For those who never give up
And such people are very few.

All These Little Things

There are lots of names on my list
Loads of faces I'm sure to remember
But I don't know when I'd see them again
Those who gave my heart warmth in December.

We look at the buildings we're leaving today
But we're taking all these little things
The memories of how we laughed together
How we walked in the corridor like kings.

There was a time
When we were partners in crime
Everybody had our names on their lips.
They said there never was
And there would never be
A gang as happening.